A ROMAN LAWYER

IN

JERUSALEM:

FIRST CENTURY.

BY

W. W. STORY.

LORING, Publisher,

BOSTON.

Price, 25 Cents.

Mrs. Whitney's best Novel,

HITHERTO:

A

STORY OF YESTERDAYS.

Rich Cloth. ***Price, $2.***

This is the unique and half mysterious title of the truly great and good book, from the pen of

MRS. A. D. T. WHITNEY,

Author of *'Faith Gartney's Girlhood,'* *'The Gayworthys,'* *'Patience Strong's Outings.'*

We do not hesitate to pronounce "Hitherto" the best work of this much-loved author. It embodies, without being dry or abstruse, a sublime philosophy of life; and to those who can appreciate its deep, earnest spirit, "Hitherto" will become a household book to cheer and encourage the darker days, and, at all times, to satisfy the soul with the grandest thought.

In this beautiful "Story of Yesterdays," Mrs. Whitney outdoes herself. It unites the insight and pure devotion of "Patience Strong," the nobility of life, and the pathos of "The Gayworthys," with the romantic charm of "Faith Gartney."

The book will tell its own story, find its own cherished place, and while away the leisure hours of thousands of readers, who will find in its pages happy dreams from the realm of romance.

A ROMAN LAWYER

IN

JERUSALEM.

FIRST CENTURY.

BY

W. W. STORY.

[*Reprinted from Blackwood.*]

LORING, Publisher,
COR. WASHINGTON AND BROMFIELD STREETS,
BOSTON.

ROCKWELL & CHURCHILL, STEREOTYPERS AND PRINTERS,
122 Washington Street, Boston.

S 7.6
S S S S...

A ROMAN LAWYER IN JERUSALEM.

FIRST CENTURY.

Marcus, abiding in Jerusalem,
Greeting to Caius, his best friend, in Rome!
Salve! these presents will be borne to you
By Lucius, who is wearied with this place,
Sated with travel, looks upon the East
As simply hateful — blazing, barren, bleak,
And longs again to find himself in Rome.
After the tumult of its streets, its trains
Of slaves and clients, and its villas cool
With marble porticoes beside the sea,
And friends and banquets, — more than all, its games, —
This life seems blank and flat. He pants to stand
In its vast circus all alive with heads
And quivering arms and floating robes, — the air
Thrilled by the roaring *fremitus* of men, —
The sunlit awning heaving overhead,

Swollen and strained against its corded veins,
And flapping out its hem with loud report,—
The wild beasts roaring from the pit below,—
The wilder crowd responding from above
With one long yell that sends the startled blood
With thrill and sudden flush into the cheeks,—
A hundred trumpets screaming,—the dull thump
Of horses galloping across the sand,—
The clang of scabbards, the sharp clash of steel,—
Live swords, that whirl a circle of gray fire,—
Brass helmets flashing 'neath their streaming hair,—
A universal tumult,—then a hush
Worse than the tumult—all eyes straining down
To the arena's pit—all lips set close—
All muscles strained,—and then that sudden yell,
Habet!—That's Rome, says Lucius: so it is!
That is, 'tis *his* Rome,—'tis not yours and mine.

And yet, great Jupiter here at my side
He stands with face aside as if he saw
The games he thus describes, and says, "That's life!
Life! life! my friend, and this is simply death!

Ah! for my Rome!" I jot his very words
Just as he utters them. I hate these games,
And Lucius knows it, yet he will go on,
And all against my will he stirs my blood;
So I suspend my letter for a while.

A walk has calmed me — I begin again —
Letting this last page, since it is written, stand.
Lucius is going; you will see him soon
In our great Forum, there with him will walk,
And hear him rail and rave against the East.
I stay behind, — for these bare silences,
These hills that in the sunset melt and burn,
This proud, stern people, these dead seas and lakes,
These sombre cedars, this intense still sky,
To me o'erwearied with Life's din and strain,
Are grateful as the solemn blank of night
After the fierce day's irritant excess;
Besides, a deep, absorbing interest
Detains me here, fills up my mind, and sways
My inmost thoughts, — has got as 'twere a gripe
Upon my very life, as strange as new.
I scarcely know how well to speak of this,

Fearing your raillery at best, — at worst
Even your contempt; yet, spite of all, I speak.

First, do not deem me to have lost my head,
Sun-struck, as that man Paulus was at Rome.
No, I am sane as ever, and my pulse
Beats even, with no fever in my blood.
And yet I half incline to think his words,
Wild as they were, were not entirely wild.
Nay, shall I dare avow it? I half tend,
Here in this place, surrounded by these men, —
Despite the jeering natural at first,
And then the pressure of my life-long thought
Trained up against it, — to excuse his faith,
And half admit the Christus he thinks God
Is, at the least, a most mysterious man.
Bear with me if I now avow so much;
When next we meet I will expose my mind,
But now the subject I must scarcely touch.

How many a time, while sauntering up and down
The Forum's space, or pausing 'neath the shade

Of some grand temple, arch, or portico,
Have we discussed some knotty point of law,
Some curious case, whose contradicting facts
Looked Janus-faced to innocence and guilt.
I see you now arresting me, to note
With quiet fervor and uplifted hand
Some subtle view or fact by me o'erlooked,
And urging me, who always strain my point
(Being too much, I know, a partisan),
To pause, and press not to the issue so,
But more apart, with less impetuous zeal,
Survey as from an upper floor the facts.

I need you now to rein me in, too quick
To ride a whim beyond the term of Truth,
For here a case comes up to which in vain
I seek the clue: you could clear up my mind:
But you are absent — so I send these notes.

The case is of one Judas, Simon's son,
Iscariot called — a Jew — and one of those
Who followed Christus, held by some a god,

But deemed by others to have preached and taught
A superstition vile, of which one point
Was worship of an ass; but this is false!
Judas, his follower, all the sect declare,
Bought by a bribe of thirty silver coins,
Basely betrayed his master unto death.
The question is, — Did Judas, doing this,
Act from base motives and commit a crime?
Or, all things taken carefully in view,
Can he be justified in what he did?

Here on the spot, surrounded by the men
Who acted in the drama, I have sought
To study out this strange and tragic case.
Many are dead, as Herod, Caiaphas,
And also Pilate, — a most worthy man,
Under whose rule, but all without his fault,
And, as I fancy, all against his will,
Christus was crucified. This I regret:
His words with me would have the greatest weight;
But Lysias still is living, an old man,
The chief of the Centurions, whose report

Is to be trusted, as he saw and heard,
Not once, but many a time and oft, this man.
His look and bearing, Lysias thus describes: —

"Tall, slender, not erect, a little bent;
Brows arched and dark; a high-ridged lofty head;
Thin temples, veined and delicate; large eyes,
Sad, very serious, seeming as it were
To look beyond you, and whene'er he spoke
Illumined by an inner lamping light, —
At times, too, gleaming with a strange wild fire
When taunted by the rabble in the streets;
A Jewish face, complexion pale but dark;
Thin, high-art nostrils, quivering constantly;
Long nose, full lips, hands tapering, full of veins;
His movements nervous: as he walked he seemed
Scarcely to heed the persons whom he passed,
And for the most part gazed upon the ground.

"As for his followers, I knew them all —
A strange, mad set, and full of fancies wild —
John, Peter, James — and Judas, best of all —
All seemed to me good men without offence, —

A little crazed, — but who is wholly sane?
They went about and cured the sick and halt,
And gave away their money to the poor,
And all their talk was charity and peace.
If Christus thought and said he was a god,
'Twas harmless madness, not deserving death.
What most aroused the wealthy Rabbis' rage
Was that he set the poor against the rich,
And cried that rich men all would go to hell,
And, worst of all, roundly denounced the priests,
With all their rich phylacteries and robes, —
Said they were hypocrites who made long prayers,
And robbed poor widows and devoured their means,
And were at best but whited sepulchres:
And this it was that brought him to the Cross.

"Those who went with him and believed in him
Were mostly dull, uneducated men,
Simple and honest, dazed by what he did,
And misconceiving every word he said.
He led them with him in a spellbound awe,
And all his cures they called miraculous.

They followed him like sheep where'er he went,
With feelings mixed of wonder, fear, and love.
Yes! I suppose they loved him, though they fled
Stricken with fear when we arrested him."

"What! all — all fled?" I asked. "Did none remain?"

"Not one," he said, "all left him to his fate.
Not one dared own he was a follower;
Not one gave witness for him of them all.
Stop! When I say not one of them, I mean
No one but Judas, — Judas, whom they call
The traitor, — who betrayed him to his death.
He rushed into the council-hall and cried,
'Tis I have sinned — Christus is innocent.'"

And here I come to what of all I've heard
Most touched me, — I for this my letter write.
Paulus, you know, had only for this man,
This Judas, words of scorn and bitter hate.
Mark now the different view that Lysias took!
When, urged by me, his story thus he told: —

"Some say that Judas was a base, vile man,
Who sold his master for the meanest bribe;
Others again insist he was most right,
Giving to justice one who merely sought
To overthrow the Church, subvert the law,
And on its ruins build himself a throne.
I, knowing Judas — and none better knew —
I, caring nought for Christus more than him,
But hating lies, the simple truth will tell.
No man can say I ever told a lie;
I am too old now to begin. Besides,
The truth is truth, and let the truth be told.
Judas, I say, alone of all the men
Who followed Christus, thought that he was God.
Some feared him for his power of miracles;
Some were attracted by a sort of spell;
Some followed him to hear his sweet, clear voice,
And gentle speaking, hearing with their ears,
And knowing not the sense of what he said;
But one alone believed he was the Lord,
The true Messiah of the Jews. That one
Was Judas, — he alone of all the crowd.

"He to betray his master for a bribe!
He last of all. I say this friend of mine
Was brave when all the rest were cowards there.

"His was a noble nature: frank and bold,
Almost to rashness bold, yet sensitive,
Who took his dreams for firm realities;
Who once believing, all in all believed;
Rushing at obstacles and scorning risk,
Ready to venture all to gain his end,
No compromise or subterfuge for him,
His act went from his thought straight to the burs;
Yet with this ardent and impatient mood
Was joined a visionary mind that took
Impressions quick and fine, yet deep as life.
Therefore it was that in this subtle soil
The master's words took root and grew and flowered.
He heard, and followed, and obeyed; his faith
Was serious, earnest, real — winged to fly;
He doubted not, like some who walked with him;
Desired no first place, as did James and John;
Denied him not with Peter: not to him

His master said, 'Away! thou'rt an offence;
Get thee behind me, Satan!' — not to him,
'Am I so long with ye who know me not?'
Fixed as a rock, untempted by desires
To gain the post of honor when his Lord
Should come to rule — chosen from out the midst
Of six-score men as his apostle — then
Again selected to the place of trust,
Unselfish, honest, he among them walked.

"That he was honest, and was so esteemed,
Is plain from this, — they chose him out of all
To bear the common purse, and take and pay.
John says he was a thief, because he grudged
The price that for some ointment once was paid,
And urged 'twere better given to the poor.
But did not Christus ever for the poor
Lift up his voice, — 'Give all things to the poor;
Sell everything and give all to the poor!'
And Judas, who believed, not made believe,
Used his own words, and Christus, who excused
The gift because of love, rebuked him not.

Thief! ay, he 'twas, this very thief, they chose
To bear the purse and give alms to the poor.
I, for my part, see nothing wrong in this."

"But why, if Judas was a man like this,
Frank, noble, honest," — here I interposed —
"Why was it that he thus betrayed his Lord?"

"This question oft did I revolve," said he,
"When all the facts were fresh, and oft revolved
In later days, and with no change of mind;
And this is my solution of the case: —

"Daily he heard his master's voice proclaim,
'I am the Lord! the Father lives in me!
Who knoweth me knows the Eternal God!
He who believes in me shall never die!
No! he shall see me with my angels come
With power and glory here upon the earth
To judge the quick and dead! Among you here
Some shall not taste of death before I come
God's kingdom to establish on the earth!'

"'What meant these words? They seethed in Judas' soul.
'Here is my God — Messias, King of kings,
Christus, the Lord — the Saviour of us all.
How long shall he be taunted and reviled,
And threatened by this crawling scum of men?
Oh, who shall urge the coming of that day
When he in majesty shall clothe himself
And stand before the astounded world its King?'
Long brooding over this inflamed his soul;
And, ever rash in schemes as wild in thought,
At last he said, 'No longer will I bear
This ignominy heaped upon my Lord.
No man hath power to harm the Almighty One.
Ay, let men's hand be lifted, then, at once,
Effulgent like the sun, swift like the sword,
The jagged lightning flashes from the cloud,
Shall he be manifest — the living God —
And prostrate all shall on the earth adore!'

"Such was his thought when at the passover
The Lord with his disciples met and supped;
And Christus saw the trouble in his mind,

And said, 'Behold, among you here is one
That shall betray me — he to whom I give
This sop;' and he the sop to Judas gave;
And added, 'That thou doest, quickly do;'
And Judas left him, hearing these last words —
'Now shall the Son of man be glorified.'

"Ah, yes! his master had divined his thought;
His master should be glorified through him.

"Straight unto me and the high priests he came,
Filled with this hope, and said, 'Behold me here,
Judas, a follower of Christus! — Come!
I will point out my master whom you seek!'
And out at once they sent me with my band;
And as we went, I said, rebuking him,
'How, Judas, is it you who thus betray
The lord and master whom you love, to death?'
And, smiling, then he answered, 'Fear you not;
Do you your duty; take no heed of me.' —
'Is not this vile?' I said; 'I had not deemed
Such baseness in you.' — 'Though it seem so now,'

2

Still smiling, he replied, 'wait till the end.'
Then turning round as to himself he said,
'Now comes the hour that I have prayed to see, —
The hour of joy to all who know the truth.'

"'Is this man mad?' I thought, and looked at him;
And, in the darkness creeping swiftly on,
His face was glowing, almost shone with light;
And rapt as if in visionary thought
He walked beside me, gazing at the sky.

"Passing at last beyond the Cedron brook,
We reached a garden on whose open gate
Dark vines were loosely swinging. Here we paused,
And lifted up our torches, and beheld
Against the blank white wall a shadowy group,
There waiting motionless, without a word:
A moment, and with rapid, nervous step
Judas alone advanced, and, as he reached
The tallest figure, lifted quick his head;
And crying, 'Master! Master!' kissed his cheek.
We, knowing it was Christus, forward pressed.

Malchus was at my side, when suddenly
A sword flashed out from one among them there,
And sheared his ear. At once our swords flashed out,
But Christus, lifting up his hand, said, 'Peace,
Sheathe thy sword, Peter — I must drink the cup.'
And I cried also, 'Peace, and sheathe your swords.'
Then on his arm I placed my hand, and said,
'In the law's name.' He nothing said, but reached
His arms out, and we bound his hands with cords.
This done, I turned, but all the rest had fled,
And he alone was left to meet his fate.

"My men I ordered then to take and bear
Their prisoner to the city; and at once
They moved away. I, seeing not our guide,
Cried, 'Judas!'—but no answer; then a groan
So sad and deep it startled me. I turned,
And there, against the wall, with ghastly face,
And eyeballs starting in a frenzied glare,
As in a fit, lay Judas; his weak arms
Hung lifeless down, his mouth half open twitched,
His hands were clutched and clenched into his robes,

And now and then his breast heaved with a gasp.
Frightened, I dashed some water in his face,
Spoke to him, lifted him, and rubbed his hands.
At last the sense came back into his eyes,
Then with a sudden spasm fled again,
And to the ground he dropped. I searched him o'er,
Fearing some mortal wound, yet none I found.
Then with a gasp again the life returned,
And stayed, but still with strong convulsion twitched.
'Speak, Judas! speak!' I cried. 'What does this mean?'
No answer! 'Speak, man!' Then at last he groaned:
'Go, leave me! leave me, Lysias. O my God!
What have I done? O Christus! Master, Lord,
Forgive me, oh, forgive me!' Then a cry
Of agony that pierced me to the heart,
As grovelling on the ground he turned away
And hid his face, and shuddered in his robes.
Was this the man whose face an hour ago
Shone with a joy so strange? What means it all?
Is this a sudden madness? 'Speak!' I cried.
'What means this, Judas? Be a man and speak!'
Yet there he lay, and neither moved nor spoke.

I thought that he had fainted, till at last
Sudden he turned, and grasped my arm, and cried,
'Say, Lysias, is this true, or am I mad?'
'What true?' I said. 'True that you seized the Lord!
You could not seize him — he is God the Lord!
I thought I saw you seize him. Yet I know
That was impossible, for he is God!
And yet you live — you live. He spared you, then.
Where am I? what has happened? A black cloud
Came o'er me when you laid your hands on him.
Where are they all? Where is he? Lysias, speak!'

"'Judas,' I said, 'what folly is all this?
Christus my men have bound and borne away;
The rest have fled. Rouse now and come with me!
My men await me, rouse yourself, and come!'

"Throwing his arms up, in a fit he fell,
With a loud shriek that pierced the silent night.
I could not stay, but, calling instant aid,
We bore him quick to the adjacent house,
And placing him in kindly charge, I left,
Joining my men who stayed for me below.

"Straight to the high priest's house we hurried on,
And Christus in an inner room we placed,
Set at his door a guard, and then came out.
After a time there crept into the hall,
Where round the blazing coals we sat, a man,
Who in the corner crouched. 'What man are you?'
Cried some one; and I, turning, looked at him.
'Twas Peter. ''Tis a fellow of that band
That followed Christus, and believed in him.'—
''Tis false!' cried Peter; — and he cursed and swore
'I know him not — I never saw the man.'
But I said nothing. Soon he went away.

"That night I saw not Judas. The next day,
Ghastly, clay-white, a shadow of a man,
With robes all soiled and torn, and tangled beard,
Into the chamber where the council sat
Came feebly staggering: scarce should I have known
'Twas Judas, with that haggard, blasted face;
So had that night's great horror altered him.
As one all blindly walking in a dream
He to the table came — against it leaned —

Glared wildly round a while; — then stretching forth
From his torn robes a trembling hand, flung down,
As if a snake had stung him, a small purse,
That broke and scattered its white coins about,
And, with a shrill voice, cried, 'Take back the purse!
'Twas not for that foul dross I did the deed —
'Twas not for that — oh, horror! not for that!
But that I did believe he was the Lord;
And that he is the Lord I still believe.
But oh, the sin! — the sin! I have betrayed
The innocent blood, and I am lost! — am lost!'
So crying, round his face his robes he threw,
And blindly rushed away; and we, aghast,
Looked round, — and no one for a moment spoke.

"Seeing that face, I could but fear the end;
For death was in it, looking through his eyes.
Nor could I follow to arrest the fate
That drove him madly on with scorpion whip.

"At last the duty of the day was done,
And night came on. Forth from the gates I went,
Anxious and pained by many a dubious thought,

To seek for Judas, and to comfort him.
The sky was dark with heavy, lowering clouds;
A lifeless, stifling air weighed on the world;
A dreadful silence like a nightmare lay
Crouched on its bosom, waiting, grim and gray
In horrible suspense of some dread thing.
A creeping sense of death, a sickening smell,
Infected the dull breathing of the wind.
A thrill of ghosts went by me now and then,
And made my flesh creep as I wandered on.
At last I came to where a cedar stretched
Its black arms out beneath a dusky rock,
And, passing through its shadow, all at once
I started; for against the dubious light
A dark and heavy mass, that to and fro
Swung slowly with its weight, before me grew.
A sick, dread sense came over me; I stopped —
I could not stir. A cold and clammy sweat
Oozed out all over me; and all my limbs,
Bending with tremulous weakness like a child's.
Gave way beneath me. Then a sense of shame
Aroused me. I advanced, stretched forth my hand,

And pushed the shapeless mass; and at my touch
It yielding swung — the branch above it creaked —
And back returning struck against my face.
A human body! Was it dead, or not?
Swiftly my sword I drew and cut it down,
And on the sand all heavily it dropped.
I plucked the robes away, exposed the face —
'Twas Judas, as I feared, cold, stiff, and dead:
That suffering heart of his had ceased to beat."

Thus Lysias spoke, and ended. I confess
This story of poor Judas touched me much.
What horrible revulsions must have passed
Across that spirit in those few last hours!
What storms, that tore up life even to its roots!
Say what you will — grant all the guilt — and still
What pangs of dread remorse — what agonies
Of desperate repentance, all too late,
In that wild interval between the crime
And its last sad atonement! — life, the while,
Laden with horror all too great to bear,
And pressing madly on to death's abyss:

This was no common mind that thus could feel —
No vulgar villain sinning for reward!

Was he a villain lost to sense of shame?
Ay, so say John and Peter and the rest;
And yet — and yet this tale that Lysias tells
Weighs with me more the more I ponder it;
For thus I put it: Either Judas was,
As John affirms, a villain and a thief,
A creature lost to shame and base at heart;
Or else, which is the view that Lysias takes,
He was a rash and visionary man,
Whose faith was firm, who had no thought of crime,
But whom a terrible mistake drove mad.

Take but John's view, and all to me is blind.
Call him a villain who, with greed of gain,
For thirty silver pieces sold his Lord.
Does not the bribe seem all too small and mean?
He held the common purse, and, were he thief,
Had daily power to steal, and lay aside
A secret and accumulating fund;
So doing, he had nothing risked of fame,

While here he braved the scorn of all the world.
Besides, why chose they for their almoner
A man so lost to shame, so foul with greed?
Or why, from some five-score of trusted men,
Choose him as one apostle among twelve?
Or why, if he were known to be so vile,
(And who can hide his baseness at all times?)
Keep him in close communion to the last?
Naught in his previous life, or acts, or words,
Shows this consummate villain that, full-grown,
Leaps all at once to such a height of crime.

Again, how comes it that this wretch, whose heart
Is cased to shame, flings back the paltry bribe?
And, when he knows his master is condemned,
Rushes in horror out to seek his death?
Whose fingers pointed at him in the crowd?
Did all men flee his presence till he found
Life too intolerable? Nay; not so!
Death came too close upon the heels of crime.
He had but done what all his tribe deemed just:
All the great mass — I mean the upper class —

The Rabbis, all the Pharisees and Priests —
Ay, and the lower mob as well who cried,
"Give us Barabbas! Christus to the cross!"
These men were all of them on Judas' side,
And Judas had done naught against the law.
Were he this villain, he had but to say,
"I followed Christus till I found at last
He aimed at power to overthrow the State.
I did the duty of an honest man.
I traitor! — you are traitors who reprove."
Besides, such villains scorn the world's reproof.

Or he might say: "You call this act a crime?
What crime was it to say I know this man?
I said no ill of him. If crime there be,
'Twas yours who doomed him unto death, not mine."

A villain was he? So Barabbas was!
But did Barabbas go and hang himself,
Weary of life, — the murderer and thief?
This coarse and vulgar way will never do.
Grant him a villain, all his acts must be
Acts of a villain; if you once admit

Remorse so bitter that it leads to death,
And death so instant on the heels of crime,
You grant a spirit sensitive to shame, —
So sensitive that life can yield no joys
To counterbalance one bad act; but then
A nature such as this, though led astray,
When greatly tempted is no thorough wretch.
Was the temptation great? Could such a bribe
Tempt such a nature to a crime like this?
I say, to me it simply seems absurd.

Peter at least was not so sensitive.
He cursed and swore, denying that he knew
Who the man Christus was; but after all
He only wept — he never hanged himself.

But take the other view that Lysias takes,
All is at once consistent, clear, complete.
Firm in the faith that Christus was his God,
The great Messiah sent to save the world,
He, seeking for a sign, — not for himself,
But to show proof to all that he was God, —
Conceived this plan, rash if you will, but grand.

"Thinking him man," he said, "mere mortal man,
They seek to seize him. I will make pretence
To take the public bribe and point him out,
And they shall go, all armed with swords and staves,
Strong with the power of law, to seize on him, —
And at their touch he, God himself, shall stand
Revealed before them, and their swords shall drop,
And prostrate all before him shall adore,
And cry, 'Behold the Lord and King of all!'"
But when the soldiers laid their hands on him,
And bound him as they would a prisoner vile,
With taunts, and mockery, and threats of death —
He all the while submitting — then his dream
Burst into fragments with a crash; aghast
The whole world reeled before him; the dread truth
Swooped like a sea upon him, bearing down
His thoughts in wild confusion. He who dreamed
To open the gates of glory to his Lord,
Opened in their stead the prison's jarring door,
And saw above him his dim dream of Love
Change to a Fury stained with blood and crime.
And then a madness seized him, and remorse
With pangs of torture drove him down to death.

Conceive with me that sad and suffering heart,
If this be true that Lysias says — Conceive!
Alas! Orestes, not so sad thy fate,
For thee Apollo pardoned, purified, —
Thy Furies were appeased, thy peace returned;
But Judas perished, tortured unto death,
Unpardoned, unappeased, unpurified.
And long as Christus shall be known of men
His name shall bear the brand of infamy,
The curse of generations still unborn.

Thus much of him: I leave the question here,
Touching on naught beyond, for Lucius waits;
I hear him fuming in the courts below,
Cursing his servants and Jerusalem,
And giving them to the infernal gods.
The sun is sinking — all thy sky's afire —
And vale and mountain glow like molten ore
In the intense full splendor of its rays.
A half-hour hence all will be dull and gray;
And Lucius only waits until the shade
Sweeps down the plain, then mounts and makes his way

On through the blinding desert to the sea,
And thence his galley bears him on to Rome.

Salve et vale! — may good fortune wait
On you and all your household! Greet for me
Titus and Livia — in a word, all friends.

W. W. S.

"Jesus answered them.
Have not I chosen you
twelve, and one of you is
a Devil. He spake of
Judas Iscariot the son
of Simon, for he it was
that should betray him,
being one of the twelve."
John 6-70&71

W. W. STORY'S REMARKABLE

POEM,

A ROMAN LAWYER IN JERUSALEM:

FIRST CENTURY.

A DEFENCE OF JUDAS ISCARIOT.

Tinted Paper. Price, 25 Cents.

The argument is very interesting ; but, on the whole, we have lost so many rascals lately, by the re-writing of History, that we are inclined to hold on to Judas.—*Hartford Courant.*

The theory of the betrayal here adopted—the DeQuincey theory—furnishes a sample of that specially modern form of humanitarianism, the desire to clear the reputation of an historical personage who has been held in abhorrence from time immemorial.

Mr. Story has not laid himself open to be attacked as one who would "white-wash" the proverbial traitor, but has simply shown, in the potent manner of psychological art, that the conduct of the personage in question admits of a charitable explanation. The Roman lawyer betrays an inclination to believe the account given him by Lysias, who figures in the Poem as an old friend of Judas, and according to whose view the Christ was betrayed by one who blundered in attempting to do a great thing. Lysias believes, in fact, that Judas, warmly devoted to his Master, and fervently convinced of his godhead, conceived the idea that if he gave Christ into the hands of his enemies, a manifestation of the Master's godhead must perforce take place, to the inevitable conviction of all witnesses ; but that, seeing no such manifestation, and finding Christ a prisoner and undone, he learned how fearful a mistake he had made, and "turned, and went and hanged himself." This position is ably sustained in matter of argument, and there is a good deal of fine writing in the Poem.

—*Tinsley's Magazine.*

ROBERT FALCONER.

By GEORGE MacDONALD, L.L.D. Rich Cloth. Price, $1.75.

We believe that MacDonald's masterwork, thus far, is *Robert Falconer.* Nowhere does this author give so completely developed a character as that of *Falconer*— no other of his books possesses so much of heroic grandeur. The sublimity, the pathos, the vivid portraiture of outward as well as inward life, heighten as the book advances.

Powerful and fascinating merely as a novel even, *Robert Falconer* possesses a still higher value in its treatment of genuine, earnest doubt.

After Falconer himself, the most interesting character in this book, and perhaps in MacDonald's writings, is that of Eric Ericson, the companion of Falconer's youth, whose mental history and early death form the most pathetic episode in our author's works. A doubter, longing to believe, but attaining only to hope, Ericson awakens a combination of admiration and sympathy not accorded to any other of MacDonald's characters, and the tragedy of his life forms a striking contrast to the triumphant epic of Falconer's.

MacDonald's higher female characters are, in general, exquisitely described, but less powerfully drawn, less completely developed, than his men. The general earnestness of tone which characterizes the book, is agreeably relieved by the flavor of comic humor imparted to it by the characters of Dooble Sanny and Shargar.—***Lippincott's Magazine.***

DAVID ELGINBROD.

By GEORGE MacDONALD, L.L.D.

One handsome 12mo. vol. Cloth. Price, $1.75.

David Elginbrod, is the first of a series of works in which MacDonald's genius finds its completest expression — works which, while vividly portraying the most varied forms of life and character, are yet more remarkable for the depth of their religious and philosophic thought, and for the spirit of truest poetry and romance which pervades them throughout. In *David Elginbrod,* the most interesting character is that of the Scottish patriarch, who gives his name to the book—a character which seems the creation even more of the heart than of the brain of MacDonald. The beauty of this portrait is indeed such as to disarm criticism upon its incompleteness, but it must be acknowledged to lack the development and vigor of several of MacDonald's later conceptions. As a Novel as a whole, it may be remarked, that perhaps none of MacDonald's works excel it in the beauty of particular passages, in tenderness of pathos and variety of interest.—***Lippincott's Magazine.***

www.ingramcontent.com/pod-product-compliance
Lightning Source LLC
LaVergne TN
LVHW011121110826
845150LV00008B/2216

* 9 7 8 1 4 1 8 1 9 5 0 9 0 *